The World Through A Child's Eyes

Michael Brasier

First Edition

The World
Through
A Child's Eyes

Michael Brasier

mRB

michael Brasier

may 19, 2006

BEA

Around The World Publications, LLC
P.O. Box 1024
Franktown, CO 80116
United States of America

© 2006 by Michael Brasier

Published by Around The World Publications, LLC
P.O. Box 1024
Franktown, CO 80116

Printed in China

Cover Design: Michael Brasier
Book Design: Michael R. Brasier
Photographs Taken: Richard L. Brasier (Michael's father)

International Standard Book Number   0-9772591-0-2

Library of Congress Control Number: 2005906572

Publisher's Cataloging-in-Publication
(Provided by Quality Books, Inc.)

Brasier, Michael R.
     The World Through A Child's Eyes / Michael Brasier — 1st Edition

> ATTENTION: SCHOOLS AND BUSINESSES
> *The World Through A Child's Eyes* copyright © 2006 by Michael R. Brasier is available at quantity discounts with bulk purchase for educational, business, or sales promotional use. For information, please write to: Michael R. Brasier, P.O. Box 1024, Franktown, Colorado 80116 or email to bbrasier@etsgroup.com.

Dedication

This book is dedicated to my family who has helped me throughout my life.

Acknowledgments

The author is grateful to the following individuals who, over the last year have provided their skills, talents, encouragement and other contributions to the completion and quality of this publication:

- Richard Brasier – My Dad
- Melonie Brasier – My Mom
- Pat Cotta – My Grandmother
- David Steiner-Otoo – Provided suggestions for publishing this book
- Jalene McFadden – Provided detailed editing and comments for this book
- Bob Davis – Martial Arts Master and Instructor
- Mrs. Wendy Craigg – Governor of The Central Bank of The Bahamas
- Dr. Andrés Córdova - Dr. Córdova is a prominent attorney in Ecuador and grandson of the previous President of Ecuador
- Mr. Ralph Montgomery – Principal at Sagewood Middle School, Parker, Colorado

Table of Contents

Introduction

My dad was the first one to come up with the idea to put all my papers into a book. After I had written over thirty stories he really helped me get serious about publishing this book, so last year I started putting it together and formatting it. After about six months of work we finally were able to get this book published. I wrote my first travel story on December 28, 1999, in South Africa when I was 6 years old. At the time I was in first grade and my teacher every week would choose some one who would pick a country to research and tell about to the rest of the class. So instead of just researching I actually went to South Africa and emailed the stories and pictures to my teacher and she would teach the class about South Africa through my stories. Since then I have been writing stories about everywhere I go.

So far, I have been to thirteen different countries around the world. These include:

• Bahamas • China (Beijing) • Ecuador (Galapagos Islands & Quito) • France (Paris) • Germany (Berlin) • Hong Kong • Mexico (Cancun & Puerto Vallarta) • New Zealand	• Scotland (not really a country – unless you ask a Scotsman) • South Africa (Cape Town & Johannesburg) • United Kingdom (London and Wales) • United States (about 25 states so far) • Zimbabwe

Some of these countries I have visited more than once.

When I first started writing these stories I had a big problem with how to connect my brain to my hand and to just write what I think or say. Normally I am very good at telling people things, but as soon as I pick up a pen and paper I can't write my own name without trouble. I have come a long way since I started writing stories when I was six years old.

Anyway enough about me and on to why should you read this book. Well, you might read this book to find out things about other countries or you might read it because you want a child's opinion on things or even because you want to know what the world is like. Even if it isn't one of those reasons I hope that you would be kind enough to try reading the first few pages. If you don't enjoy the book please let me know (you can also let me know if you did enjoy reading this book).

I decided to write this book and so far it has been very fun and my father says that once I get this book out I would hopefully start liking to write more.

I started writing when I was five years old, but before that I had traveled to New Zealand, Scotland, and throughout Europe. My adventures around the world have taught me to appreciate what we have in the United States. I have also gotten a first hand look at many other people and cultures around the world and found that most people are not much different from us. For example, normally if you think of the people in China you think everyone there is evil, but when I went there the people were very friendly. It just goes to show you how people change things around to fit their own view.

I think my favorite place is South Africa because we got to see a lot of it and really got to know the people. We were there for about a month and we had a lot of fun. We saw one of the seven-natural wonders of the world in South Africa and went to a prison named Robben Island where Nelson Mandela was imprisoned.

My second favorite location that I have been is the Bahamas, were I first learned to snorkel with Flying Cloud Sailing. Also, in the Bahamas I went to a local school for three weeks and participated in a Christmas play.

I hope you enjoy reading this book and learn a little about the world that we all live in, at least about the place that I have had a chance to travel to.

South Africa
December 28, 1999

How I Got to South Africa

I flew on an airplane from Denver to Miami, Florida. I then flew from Miami to Cape Town, South Africa. This flight was fourteen hours long. I left Miami at 5:00 in the afternoon and arrived the next day at 2:00 in the afternoon.

I got dinner and breakfast on the plane, but I was asleep and missed breakfast. I watched the movies Jack Frost and Inspector Gadget on the airplane.

The airplane shook when we crossed over the equator. My dad told me that was because the winds on each side of the equator blow in different directions.

I have included two pictures below of me and my sister, Samantha, with a parrot in Miami at the hotel.

Cape Town

Cape Town is on the very tip of South Africa. It is the most southern location in all of Africa.

It is night in South Africa when it is daytime in Colorado. This is because South Africa is on the other side of the world (the time difference between Denver and South Africa is more than nine hours).

There was a very rocky beach in front of the hotel I stayed at (see pictures below). The water in Cape Town is very cold. This is the Atlantic Ocean. I saw Table Mountain in Cape Town. This is a very famous mountain that looks like the top has been cut off.

It is summer in South Africa. This is because South Africa is in the southern hemisphere of the Earth and has opposite seasons than we do. The weather in Cape Town was very nice (about 80F or 27C - Fahrenheit and Centigrade).

They do not drive on the same side of the road that we do in the United States. They drive on the left side of the road and the steering wheel in the car is on the right side of the car.

There is a large boat harbor in Cape Town. There are a lot of different types of boats, such as sail boats, power boats, and large ships.

Robben Island

I got on a boat to get to Robben Island. The boat ride took about thirty minutes. Pictures of the boat are included below.

Robben Island was a famous prison island (similar to Alcatraz in San Francisco). Robben Island was used to imprison "political prisoners". Political prisoners believe in a different way of running the country. The political prisoners in South Africa believed that blacks should have equal rights and South Africa should be a democratic country – a free country.

The prisoners on Robben Island did not have names. Instead, they were given numbers. This took away their identity. It was often very cold on the island in winter and a lot of the prisoners got very sick and died.

There were four cell blocks in the prison, A block, B block, C block, and D block. A block was used for new prisoners. B block was for leaders of the political prisoners. C block was for torturing prisoners. D block was for everyone else.

Guard Tower at Robben Island Prison

Nelson Mandela was imprisoned on Robben Island for 18 years. His jail cell was #5. I got to go into his jail cell (see picture below). When Nelson Mandela was set free in 1991 he then ran for and was elected President of South Africa. He was the first democratically elected President in the history of South Africa. He served as President for eight years. A lot of the other political prisoners have also become leaders of South Africa. Their political beliefs and ideas are being put into place today. Their fight for their ideas was worth the effort and difficulties they had to go through.

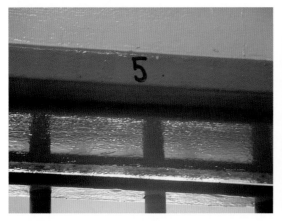 

Nelson Mandela started a rock pile at the quarry after the prison was closed in 1991. At the rock quarry where the prisoners worked, Nelson Mandela placed a rock to remember all of those that were imprisoned on Robben Island. The other former prisoners that came back to Robben Island have also added rocks to the pile. This rock pile serves as a monument to all of the prisoners of Robben Island.

Robben Island is now a museum and is a place where people can come to look at the prison cells. Robben Island now honors all the many people once imprisoned there and the strength of the human spirit.

Table Top Mountain as Seen from Robben Island

Elephant Park

January 01, 2000

We went to an Elephant Park in South Africa.

There were three elephants. Their names were Harry, Sally, and Duma. Duma was the smallest elephant. Harry was the biggest elephant. Sally was in between.

When we got to the Elephant Park they were playing in the water.

I got to feed the elephants by hand. I fed them special elephant food that we bought at the Elephant Park.

Cango Caves

January 08, 2000

I went to the Cango Caves in South
Africa. It was cold in the caves. The
temperature always stays the same
in the caves - about 18 degrees
Centigrade or 65 degrees
Fahrenheit.

There were stalactites and stalagmites in the caves. My favorite stalactite was
one that looks like a head. Water that dripped down created the stalactites and
stalagmites in the caves. A stalactite is hanging from the ceiling and a stalagmite
rises from the floor of a cavern and is caused by the water dripping down the
stalatite. Stalagmites and stalactites are often found in pairs. It takes millions of
years to make the stalactites and stalagmites.

The Cango Caves were very large. There are six sets of caves in the Cango
Caves. The Cango Caves are about five miles deep. Most of Cango Caves
have still not been explored.

Lion Park

January 08, 2000

We went to the lion park near Johannesburg, South Africa. The lions sleep twenty hours each day. There was one male in each group of lions. There were a lot of females in each group of lions. A group of lions is called a pride.

I got to pet real lion cubs. They were playful. There were about ten lion cubs.

We saw springboks. Springboks are a kind of antelope and they are the name of the South African Rugby and Cricket teams. Springboks are very colorful.

Rhino Park
January 08, 2000

We went to the Rhino Park near Johannesburg, South Africa.

We saw hippos in the pond. They have to come up to the surface for air every few minutes. We only saw their noses and the top of their heads.

We also saw water buffalos. They like water. They have very large horns. They are very big animals.

We also saw rhinos. We were very close to them (about ten feet away). They have very large horns. They are bigger than a water buffalo. There was a baby rhino. Rhinos like the mud and the water because it helps cool them off. Rhinos eat grass and other plants.

We also saw wild dogs. The wild dogs were hiding and they were sleeping when we got there. We made the car squeak and they woke up. There were about twenty wild dogs. They then began to yip and run around. They were spotted and brownish gray.

The cheetahs were on top of the hill near the fence. There were five cheetahs. They were looking at some sheep on the other side of the fence. The cheetah can run very fast. They are the fastest animal in the world. They can run up to 110 kilometers per hour (this is about 70 mph). The cheetahs are brown, black and white and they have spots. This helps them blend in with the grass. The black lines on their faces are called tear lines. These lines help the cheetah line up with its prey when it is running very fast. The cheetah hunts and kills antelope, zebras and other small animals. Their long tails help them steer when they are running very fast. Cheetahs were looking very strange at us. We were only about five or six feet away from them.

Pilansburg Game Reserve

January 15, 2000

I went on a safari at the Pilansburg Game Reserve near Sun City in South Africa. Safari is a Swahili word meaning "trip" and usually is a trip to see animals. I rode in a big safari truck.

I saw a lot of zebra. Their black and white stripes make it hard for a blood-sucking fly to see them. All zebra's stripes are not the same. Every zebra has it's own stripe pattern; just like people's fingerprints, every one is different.

I saw a lot of white rhinos. There are two kinds of rhinos. There are white rhinos and black rhinos. The black rhinos are an endangered species. This means that there are not very many black rhinos left. One of the rhinos I saw was bleeding from a fight with another rhino.

I saw a lot of wildebeest. They look kind of like a water buffalo. They look very funny.

I saw a lot of giraffes. They have really long necks so they can reach very high leaves on the trees.

I saw a lot of elephants. We got very close to one elephant. The elephant was almost rubbing against the truck we were riding in. Elephants flap their ears to keep cool and give off body heat. An elephant is bigger than a rhino.

I saw a lot of antelope. We saw many types of antelope. One kind is called a Springbok. Another kind of antelope is called a Kudu.

I saw a leopard. The leopard looks a little like a cheetah. It is bigger than a cheetah, but the cheetah is much faster.

On my trip to South Africa I got to see what is called "The Big Five". The Big Five are; elephant, rhino, lion, leopard, and water buffalo.

I almost fell asleep on the safari.

Victoria Falls in Zimbabwe

January 10, 2000

We went to Victoria Falls in Zimbabwe. We saw people bungee jumping. There are seven waterfalls in Victoria Falls.

There was mist coming from the waterfalls. The mist from the waterfalls and the sun creates a lot of rainbows.

Victoria Falls is one of the seven natural wonders of the world. Victoria Falls is one the of natural wonders of the world because it is the widest falls on earth and has the most water going over it.

We went on a helicopter ride in Zimbabwe. We flew over Victoria Falls. The waterfalls looked very big from above. I saw a colorful rainbow. The mist from the falls and the sun creates a lot of rainbows around Victoria Falls. Victoria Falls is called "the smoke that thunders" by the local people. This is because the mist looks like smoke and the water is very loud.

The helicopter ride was about fifteen minutes long. In addition to the falls, I saw a lot of rhinos and water buffalo from the air. I almost feel asleep on the helicopter ride.

David Livingstone found Victoria Falls in 1855. Livingstone was a Scotsman and a combination of missionary, doctor, explorer, scientist and anti-slavery activist. He spent thirty years in Africa, exploring almost one third of the continent. In 1871 journalist Henry Stanley greeted him with the now famous words: "Dr Livingstone, I presume?".

I also learned that one of the most dangerous animals in Africa is also one of the smallest animals. It is a mosquito. A mosquito can carry a disease called malaria that can kill people. We had to get shots and take pills to keep from getting malaria.

Washington DC – Our Nation's Capital
December 30, 2000

I got to go to Washington DC to see some of the sites in our nation's capital.

The first site I saw was the Lincoln Memorial. This was built to honor President Lincoln, our sixteenth President of the United States of America. President Lincoln is important because he freed the black people from being slaves to the white people.

Then, we walked to the Vietnam Memorial. It was built in honor of the people who died in the Vietnam War. It has the names of over 50,000 people that died written on the wall. My dad was in the Air Force fixing planes during the Vietnam War. My dad had friends that died in the war.

Then we drove down the road to the Washington Monument. It was built in honor of President Washington, the first President of the Unites States of America. The Monument is over 360 feet tall and is sort of a peach color. The Monument also has American flags all around it.

Then we drove to the Smithsonian Air and Space Museum. It had spacecraft and airplanes, including the first airplane flown by the Wright Brothers in 1903. There were a lot of different sections in the museum that you could go to learn about flying. I saw the largest rocket ever built, the Saturn 5, and I saw spacecraft that landed on the moon in 1969.

We went to the nation's capital were people elected to Congress meet and make the laws that we all live by. We also drove by the National Christmas Tree, which the President of the United States lights each year.

We then walked to the White House and took a few pictures. The White House is where the President of the United States lives. Currently, President Clinton lives in the White House, however, President Bush will move into the White House in a few weeks.

All in all, I really enjoyed the trip and seeing some of the sites in Washington DC. This trip taught me a little bit about our nation's history and our country's capital city.

Spring Break in the Bahamas

March 26-31, 2001

I would like to tell you about the Bahamas during spring break 2001. The Bahamas is located fifty miles off the coast of Florida and has more than seven hundred islands in the country. We, my dad and I, went to the island of New Providence and the city of Nassau, the capital of the country. We stayed at the British Colonial Hilton, which used to be called Fort Nassau. The Bahamas could be considered "living islands", because they are made up of almost entirely the skeletons of once living organisms.

The Bahamas used to be a British colony, but became a free country in 1961. The two main types of businesses in the Bahamas are tourism and banking/finance. There are more than four hundred banks in the Bahamas. Diving, snorkeling, swimming with sharks, swimming with dolphins, snorkeling with stingrays, barefoot sailing, water skiing, parasailing, and ocean kayaking are a few of the things you can do in the Bahamas.

I went on a sailboat called the Riding High. It is 56 feet long and we sailed to Rode Island. We snorkeled and saw two reefs. At the second reef we got a clamshell that had both sides still together. The shell was white and bumpy. It was fun snorkeling! We had a BBQ on the boat. I ate everything and then we sailed all the way back to New Providence island and we had a great day!

Friday we went to Atlantis. It is a major hotel on Paradise Island. We walked about fifteen miles that day. We walked all the way to the Atlantis hotel and through the casino. We saw a huge crystal in the middle of a room. There is a huge aquarium at Atlantis that you can walk though. The aquarium had a lot of fish and stingrays. We also saw really large manta ray swimming in the aquarium. The manta ray was about 6 feet across. Manta rays are a large type of stingray and have two large flaps on the front that look like horns. However, these two flaps are used to collect small particles of food called plankton. Manta rays are very graceful and beautiful animals.

Saturday, March 31, we went to Sting Ray City located on Blue Lagoon Island. We got to snorkel with real stingrays. There is a huge stingray call Stumpy, because it has a very short tail. It is the biggest stingray I have ever seen. We got to feed the stingrays small pieces of

squid. A stingray eats by sucking food into its mouth which is located on the bottom of its body. A stingray does not have any teeth, but can suck in food five times stronger than a vacuum cleaner. I got to pet and hold a white stingray call Angel. This white stingray is a very rare type of stingray. I was the first person to find Angel lying on the bottom buried in the sand. It is very cool to swim with stingrays. They are gentle animals. Stingrays are my favorite sea animal. Afterwards, we went to the beach and the water was a lot shallower then I thought it would be.

I really enjoyed my trip to the Bahamas. I got to do a lot of exciting things. I hope others also get to enjoy these exciting experiences.

China
April 24 – May 08, 2001

The Differences Between China and the USA

I recently took a trip to China and I would like to tell you about the differences between China and the United States that I have seen during my travels. China is actually called the People's Republic of China (PRC). Mao Tse-Tung established the PRC in 1949. Before the PRC was created, China was ruled by Emperors and had a very long history consisting of many different dynasties over the last 4000 years, such as the Jin Dynasty, the Yuan Dynasty, the Ming Dynasty, and the Quin Dynasty.

The capital of the People's Republic of China is Beijing. The People's Republic of China is a communist country. That means that the government controls what your job is, where you live, who the rulers of the country are, and many other aspects of people's lives. The United States is a democracy, which means that we choose where we live, we choose our jobs, and we choose our rulers, including the President.

The Chinese believe in many different religions. The major religion is Buddhism, which is where people believe in Buddha (their God and their savior). The other major religion in China is Daoism, although I do not know anything about this religion.

The food is different in China. It is good for you and it makes you feel good. I really liked the food we ate. At some of the street food stands you can get just about anything you want to eat. Most of the food at these stands is served on sticks. You can get beef, chicken, pork, squid, octopus, bananas, strawberries, kiwi, crickets, grasshoppers, beetles, and even scorpions. I tried a lot of different things, but I admit that I did not try everything.

The Chinese have different looks than my family and I do. They have black hair, white skin, and red freckles. Their eyes are also different. Their eyes are slanted, while our eyes are round.

The Chinese have a different language than we do. There are many different Chinese languages in China with many different dialects. A lot of the Chinese that we talked to we could not understand. I did learn two Chinese words that helped me communicate. "Nee-how" which means hello and "sia-si" which means thank you. The Chinese also read from right to left, unlike we do from left to right. The Chinese written symbols stand for words and sounds, instead of letters like our alphabet. Chinese symbols often look like the word or sound they represent; such as bamboo may be straight lines that look like bamboo.

In China you must ask the government permission to have a baby. I did not understand this, but it is the law. If you get permission to have a baby, you can only have one baby your entire life. This was a shocker to me!

I was very surprised by two things during my visit to China. 1) The people here are very, very friendly, and 2) they are extremely fascinated by small children from the United States. Everywhere we went crowds of people mobbed us wanting to see us, touch us, and take our pictures. In one afternoon, Samantha (my sister – three years old) and I had our pictures taken over one hundred times by different people. They were also amazed when they saw my baby sister Stephanie! They could not believe we had a five-month-old baby out and about. I am not sure exactly what the fascination was, but we were told by a number of local Chinese that 1) they thought we were very cute, 2) they were amazed that we had three children in our family, and 3) they do not take babies out of the home until they are at least one year old. Seeing a baby as small as my sister Stephanie was a big surprise to them. They absolutely loved my other sister Samantha; they kind of treated her like a little Panda bear and everyone wanted their picture with her.

The young teenage girls seemed to really like me and they would mob me and want their pictures taken with me. Even when we went to major tourist sites like the Forbidden City or the Great Wall, we seemed to become the attraction. We often had to keep moving so we would not get mobbed. We had up to one hundred people surrounding us at one time wanting to take pictures with us.

I would not like to live in China; it is too crowded. I hope everyone gets the opportunity to travel to China and experience this interesting country.

Great Wall of China

I would like to tell you about my trip to the Great Wall of China. The Great Wall, also known as the "Ten Thousand Li Great Wall," was built to keep invaders out of China. Building on the wall began over 2,500 years ago. The Great Wall is over 4,000 kilometers long (2,500 miles – almost the distance from San Francisco to New York City). The Great Wall is the only man-made structure that can be seen from outer space. It is made of stone and brick.

Various rulers and emperors in China initially built the Great Wall in small sections to protect their territories. The Ming Dynasty, 1368 – 1644 AD, and the Qing Dynasty, 1644 – 1911 AD, made the most progress on linking all of the sections together to form one continuous wall. The People's Republic of China (PRC) has done a lot of work on restoring and fixing the wall.

I got to climb up a section of the Great Wall to one of the towers. The steps are very steep and wide. I climbed 462 steps up to one of the towers with my sister, Samantha, and my dad.

The Great Wall is about 8 meters (26 feet) tall and about 7 meters (21 feet) wide. The Great Wall goes over hills and mountains throughout China.

The Great Wall has become one of the most well known symbols of China.

Forbidden City

The Forbidden City is also called the Imperial Palace.

The Forbidden City was built in 1511, almost 500 years ago, during the Ming Dynasty, 1368 – 1644 AD, and the Qing Dynasty, 1644 – 1911 AD. That is a very old city. There were twenty-four emperors who lived in the city. The Forbidden City was considered a "golden prison" because the emperors could not leave the city and were always watched over and taken care of. This was because the emperors were considered gods.

Tien An Men Square

Tien An Men Square is the place where Mao Tse-Tung declared China a communistic country and created the People's Republic of China (PRC) in 1949. Tien An Men Square is a very large area that can hold over one million people. A lot of meetings and parades are held in the square.

On June 4, 1989 a group of students held a protest against communism in Tien An Men Square. The PRC government ordered them to stop, but they did not. The PRC then ordered in the army and tanks. The PRC government crushed some of the students with the tanks and arrested the other students.

Hong Kong

On my recent trip to China I visited Hong Kong which is a group of islands in Asia in the South China Sea on the southern coast of mainland China. The recent history of Hong Kong goes back to the 1840's; however, Hong Kong has a long and rich history that goes back over 6,000 years.

Hong Kong has become important to the world because of its shipping industry. Hong Kong is the largest shipping port in the world and handles more shipping containers than any other shipping port. Hong Kong is also considered a bridge between Asia in the east and the western countries, i.e. United States...

In the late 1600's, China and Britain established a shipping trade industry. British traders began to illegally ship thousands of crates of opium (a powerful drug) to China. In 1839 the first war between Britain and the Chinese began; this was known as the Opium War. To end this war, China ceded Hong Kong to the British. In 1898 a treaty was established in which Hong Kong, and the surrounding islands, were leased to Britain for 99 years. Britain established Hong Kong as an industrial, commercial and shipping port. Britain returned Hong Kong to China on 30 June 1997. China then established Hong Kong as a Special Administrative Region (SAR). SAR means that Hong Kong keeps its capitalist government, but future heads of Hong Kong must be Chinese residents.

Currently, Hong Kong has 6.5 million people packed into only 300 square kilometers (116 square miles). When you visit Hong Kong you see lots of high rises to house all of those people in such a small space. The Hong Kong people speak both Chinese and English. The three most common religions are Daoism, Buddhism, and Confucianism. In Hong Kong people still practice acupuncture. This is where needles are used to relive pain and cure illnesses.

In Hong Kong they have different food. They eat Chinese dumplings, duck is common, and they have rice with everything. A dumpling is dough that is cooked over meat stuffing. It can be steamed, fried, or baked. They have duck and it is as common as chicken is in the States. Duck is a popular food. Rice is served with every meal.

Hong Kong is rich in history and is an important city to the world. For people wanting to travel to China, Hong Kong acts as a gateway into this country and provides access to a very different part of the world.

All About San Francisco

June 24 – 29, 2001

I want to tell you a little about San Francisco and a number of areas that are around the San Francisco bay area. First I would like to tell you about Bodega Bay. Bodega Bay is north of San Francisco about one to two hour drive from the Golden Gate Bridge. We got some fresh, live crab at the fish market. The person who got the crab used hotdog tongs to get the crabs out of the tank they were in and put them into a bucket to take them to a scale and weigh them. He told us to keep the crabs out of water and wind because in the water they will breathe all of the oxygen and in wind their lungs will dry out. I got to carry the LIVE crabs back to the RV, I was a little nervous about that.

Now I would like to tell you about the wine country. There are two main valleys in the wine country, Napa Valley and Sonoma Valley that are north of San Francisco. That is where most of the wine is made in America. It had the

most grapes I have ever seen. Did you know there are more than one thousand different kinds of wines? That is because of time, different grapes and wood the grapes are aged in. Just like if you leave a glass of grape juice out for a period of time the sugar will turn into alcohol. Wooden barrels are used make different tastes of wine and there are different ingredients that are put into the barrels with the grape juice. Different lengths of time will make different amounts of

alcohol and vary the taste of the wine. You first smell the wine to tell the difference between wines. Champagne is one kind of wine that I know very well.

We visited six different wineries in Napa and Sonoma. We went to Domaine Chandon, Robert Mondavi, Grich Hills, Beringer, Foia a Duex, and Viansa. My

The World Through A Child's Eyes

favorite winery was Viansa because they also had a lot of gourmet food to eat, which gave me something to do since I could not taste the wine.

Next is the Golden Gate Bridge in San Francisco. It is so tall that when the fog comes rolling in the towers are the only part still visible. The bridge is called the Golden Gate Bridge because it is orange, but looks gold from a distance with the sun shining on it. The engineer who built the Golden Gate Bridge was named Joseph Strauss. It took 20 years to perfect the Golden Gate Bridge. The bridge was opened in 1937. The Golden Gate Bridge has become the symbol of San Francisco.

Next is the football field, one of the original athletic parks. It was not only a football field, but also a baseball field. The teams that played there are the San Francisco 49ers (football) and the San Francisco Giants (baseball). The stadium was originally called Candlestick Park, but the name was changed to 3Com Park a few years ago. The stadium seats more than 50,000 people, not including the teams.

Now I would like to tell you about Coit Tower. It was built in honor of Lilly Hitchcock Coit. It was called Coit Tower because her last name was Coit and she was a fan of firefighters. She joined the Knickerbocker Engine Company No. 5 and she wore a badge that the firemen gave her. The tower was built in 1937 to represent a fire hose nozzle and is 210 feet tall.

Now we turn our attention to Alcatraz Island. Alcatraz was the site of a U.S. Army prison in the Civil War. In 1934 Alcatraz was turned into a maximum-security prison and housed some of the most dangerous criminals in the world. It has not been used as a prison since 1963. No one ever escaped from Alcatraz. There was one man on Alcatraz who studied birds and became an expert on them. He wrote books and papers about birds. He was called the

30

"Birdman of Alcatraz". The nickname of Alcatraz is "The Rock". There was a movie made called "The Rock" that was about Alcatraz.

Now for Fisherman's Wharf. It is filled with Dungeness Crab, mouth-watering isn't it? The crabs are fresh and you can buy then with abalone, a shellfish that is becoming extinct. You can also get a number of types of fish on Fisherman's Wharf, shrimp, abalone, sea bass, squid, salmon, mackerel, and cod. The area is lined with fine seafood restaurants. We had dinner on Fisherman's Wharf and I had Dungeness Crab and Fettuccine Alfredo.

San Francisco is one of the most beautiful cities in the world. The bridges, buildings, and interesting people make it a wonderful place to visit. I would strongly recommend that you visit this wonderful city.

Crazy Horse Memorial
September 07, 2001

The Crazy Horse memorial is a large Indian monument that is being built in South Dakota showing an Indian Chief named Crazy Horse pointing and saying "My land is where my dead lay buried".

The Crazy Horse memorial is 563 feet tall from the bottom of Crazy Horse to the top of his feather. His outreached hand is 641 ft long. Crazy Horse is more than a carving; it is a monument to honor the American Indians.

This will be done with an Indian museum, medical training center and University.

The Crazy Horse memorial is located in Custer, South Dakota. The Indians picked this location because it was their homeland and sacred land.

Crazy Horse was an Indian chief who died in a battle over the Indian's land at age 35. He protected his tribe in the only manner he knew and he died of a stabbing in the back by a U.S. Army soldier in a battle on September 6, 1877.

The man that started the Crazy horse sculpture was Korczak. Korczak was asked to carve the memorial by Henry Standing Bear because Korczak's birthday is on the same day that Crazy Horse died and the Indians believe there is a link between them. The Indians and Korczak decided on a carving because Crazy Horse had told his people that he would return to them in stone one day.

Mr. Korczak visited the Black Hills and Chief Henry Standing Bear for the first time in 1940. In 1945, five years after his first visit, Mr. Korczak decided to do the Indian memorial. Korczak arrived at the Crazy Horse site when he was 38. The first blast was on October 20, 1982.

Korczak funded the memorial privately and twice turned the government down for funding. He wanted the memorial to become a tribute to the Indians and felt that because the government had betrayed the Indian people it was not right for him to accept the government funding. He was also concerned that if the government funded it it would never be finished

The Crazy Horse memorial has been in the making for more than thirty years and will continue for many, many more. The size of the sculpture and the building of the surrounding facilities are going to take a very long time. Korczak, because he knew it would take so long, wrote detailed instructions and drawings for his sculpture so the work could continue after his death. After Korczak died his children have seen that his work continues.

I think that Crazy Horse memorial is a very nice way for the white people to recognize that the Indians have heroes too. I feel that the white man mistreated the Indians. I enjoyed learning about Crazy Horse and his people.

Mount Rushmore

September 08, 2001

Mount Rushmore is located in Keystone, South Dakota in the Black Hills. This location was chosen because it is one of the oldest regions of North America. The first location for Mount Rushmore was on the side of a mountain that had too much bad weather and they only went down one foot and found bad rock. So they relocated the sculpture to Keystone, South Dakota.

Mount Rushmore was built to put South Dakota on the map because the people felt that they did not have anything drawing visitors to their state. They wanted to increase the visibility of their State.

Mount Rushmore is 180 feet tall and 200 feet long. It consists of the heads of George Washington, Teddy Roosevelt, Thomas Jefferson and Abraham Lincoln. It looks like they are sticking their heads out of a rock.

Gutzon Borglum, the designer of Mount Rushmore, was born a son of Danish Mormons in Idaho in 1867. Borglum studied art in Paris. In 1915 Gutzon Borglum began the Mount Rushmore Memorial. Searching for the site and getting funding were the major problems he encountered along the way.

Mount Rushmore was started in 1927 and it took two years just to find the mountain to carve. It was completed in 1941. Only six and one half years were spent on actual carving.

Borglum chose George Washington because he is the founding father of our country. Teddy Roosevelt was chosen because he was the protector of the working man. Thomas Jefferson was chosen because he expanded the country. Abraham Lincoln was chosen because he preserved the Union.

Mount Rushmore was almost not completed because the government ran out of funding for the project. During the creation of Mount Rushmore workers had to use dynamite and hand tools to carve the mountain. Several times they had to change the plans of the sculptor because they would run into bad rock.

When I think of Mount Rushmore I feel a lot of pride in my country and the things we stand for. I feel that our country stands for freedom for all and that is very important.

Note: My trip to Mount Rushmore was only three days before the 911 attacks in New York City and Washington DC. I think about Mount Rushmore often and what that monument and this country stand for. I am proud to be an American!

Kennedy Space Center
January 31, 2002

I had the opportunity to visit the Kennedy Space Center. The Kennedy Space Center (KSC) is located on Merritt Island, Florida. Its purpose is to launch shuttles and satellites into space, which is a big job. All American manned space flights have been launched from Kennedy Space Center.

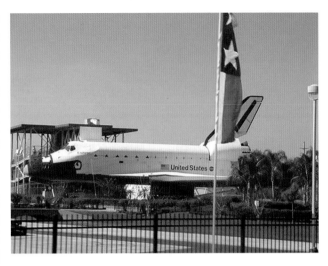

The history of space flight started in the 1950's when the Russians sent a satellite into space called Sputnik. The Americans did not like the Russian satellite going over them and so we started the "space race". The American manned space programs were called; Freedom, Mercury, Gemini, and Apollo. The first American in space was Alan Sheppard as part of Project Mercury. His launch was on May 5, 1961.

The most famous space mission was Apollo 11. The final countdown has just started at five minutes. The liquid hydrogen had set over night and the ship seemed to come alive as the ice fell off in the gleaming sun in the early day. At one minute, everyone was hoping and praying that the rocket would liftoff to the moon. Final five seconds, 4, 3, 2, 1, blastoff. The windows rattled as the ice fell off the rocket. It finally happened, the rocket blasts off to the moon.

As part of the Apollo 11 mission, Neil Armstrong was the first man to step onto the moon on July 20, 1969. His historic words were, "One small step for man, one giant leap for mankind".

Neil Armstrong and Buzz Aldrin brought back the first pieces of the moon when they splashed down in the Pacific Ocean and were picked up by Navy ships.

The layout of KSC consists of the VAB, the OMB, and the launch pads. First there is the VAB, the Vehicle Assembly Building which is where they put the Shuttle together. The OMB is the Orbiter Maintenance Building where they make sure everything on the Orbiter is in order, everything is working correctly, and test the Orbiter for leaks.

The Launch Pad consists of two parts, the crawler and the launch site. The crawler is the transporter that takes the Shuttle to the launch site. It is probably the hardest job because it takes six hours to get to the launch site. It travels at a maximum speed of one mile per hour. The crawler looks like a giant pad with treads. It also is the launch pad that the Shuttle launches off of at the launch site. The launch site is the place where they fill the Shuttle with fuel and liquid hydrogen and launch the Orbiter.

The launch consists of five steps. The first step is preparing the Shuttle for launch. This consists of building the shuttle, painting the shuttle, and testing the shuttle. They also have to assemble the boosters, fuel tanks, and Orbiter together with the Shuttle. Then they transport the Shuttle from the VAB to the crawler to the launch site.

Now the moment everyone waits for, which consists of two steps. The launch prep is where they hookup the air, electricity and liquid hydrogen. Then they start the countdown, final ten seconds, 10, 9, 8, a rain of silence, 4, 3, 2, 1, blast-off and they are off into the blue sky. Next thing they know the astronauts are in space. Their mission can be many things. It can be testing, working, or doing scientific things.

The landing of the Shuttle is usually in California because they do not want risk an accident at KSC and possibly shut down the launch site, which makes sense.

Sometime in the future NASA wants to have a manned mission to Mars. This should be launched in next ten years because they want to have everything perfect for the mission. Also, they have to make the Shuttle for the mission.

NASA is also working on the International Space Station, which should be up and working in the next year, which is a stretch. The International Space Station will be used to conduct experiments and then become a home for people who will be going to the moon or Mars. The International Space Station is over 360 feet in width and over two football fields long. It is so big that it is visible from Earth.

I hope you get the opportunity to visit the Kennedy Space Center because it is a national landmark of what Americans have been able to accomplish. I hope to be part of the NASA space program one day and possibly even the first person to step on Mars.

The Bahamas
November 09, 2002

I would like to tell you about my most recent stay in the Bahamas. Last time I was in the Bahamas it was for one week, this time it was for three weeks and it was much different.

If you were wondering where the Bahamas are, they are about 80 miles off the coast of Florida and near Cuba. There are about 700 islands that make up the Bahamas. I've only been to four of them: New Providence, Rose Island, Blue Lagoon, and Paradise Island. That's only 0.3 % of the islands; that's too little for me. I'm going to see 10.0 % of them before I die, I hope. There are only about 100 islands that are big; the rest aren't well known. The biggest island is Andros.

The government of the Bahamas consists of three branches. The first is the Executive branch, which consists of the Chief of State, who is the Queen of England and is represented by the Governor General, and the Prime Minister, and the appointed Cabinet members. Second is the Legislative branch which consists of the Senate and the House of Assembly. The Legislative branch makes the laws for the people of the Bahamas. Third is the Judiciary branch, an independent judiciary is provided for under the constitution, along with the right of appeal to her majesty's privy council in England.

Now about the people of the Bahamas, most of them seem very greedy, but there are some that are nice like a guy who helped my mom back to the hotel. It started when my mom went to the laundry mat and the taxi driver was very greedy so my mom finished the laundry and started walking back to the hotel. A guy in a pick-up truck stopped and drove her back to the hotel and he wouldn't take any money for helping her. Now what about the greedy people, like this taxi driver who wouldn't take a hint he kept rounding people up to get more money he was the greediest man I ever met, in fact, my dad almost got in a fight with him.

Now about the weather in the Bahamas. If you think you have a light winter think of 70 to 80 degrees temperature in the winter time in the Bahamas. Where I come from there is six feet of snow in the winter. That's harsh for me, don't you think so!

The banking is different in the Bahamas as well, For instance, on the paper money the queen is on the front and shells on the back. If you have some US dollars in the Bahamas that's fine because you can use them too, as well as Bahamian dollars. That is nice for tourists, and when you come home I think you should save the dollars you get in the Bahamas because I have a feeling you will be back to the Bahamas soon; and if you don't that might be a good thing to pass down to your children and they pass down to there children and on and on. Did you know that there are about 350 different banks in the Bahamas? That is a lot! Did you know that I know the Deputy Governor of the Central Bank of The Bahamas? Her name is Mrs. Craigg or that's what I refer to her as; you might address her differently. Mrs. Craigg is a very nice person. I hope I see her again soon. I don't know her husband since he couldn't make it to the dinner that my dad, mom, sisters, and I had with her. My baby sister got so attached to Mrs. Craigg that we literally had to pull her away from Mrs. Craigg. I know you think that someone set this up but no one did and Mrs. Craigg started to cry. Now that's sensitive, don't you think so?

The hotels are very nice in the Bahamas the Hilton is good, but the Atlantis is perfect for the family. The hotel is fantastic and the dining is the best on the island. The pool is great for children and the slides are really nice. The great ones are the Tube Slide and the Challenger. Do not go on the Leap of Faith – you will shake for a day and a half if you do. The Jungle Slide is good for beginners and there are slides for little ones too. Over all I give the Atlantis a 5-star rating.

I got to try scuba diving in the swimming pool at the hotel while we were in the Bahamas. I was actually too young to take lessons (I was only nine years old and you are supposed to be ten), but the instructor let me put on the tanks and swim around the bottom of the pool for awhile. I REALLY enjoyed scuba diving. I hope to get my scuba diving certification some day.

I hope you hade a great time reading this story with me.

Dolphin Encounters in the Bahamas

October 22 – November 09, 2002

I would like to tell you about a place called "Dolphin Encounters". The last time I did a Dolphin Encounter in January 2002 it was fun, but this time I did something different. It was called "Swim with the Dolphins" which is what I am going to talk about in this paper. I hope you have as much fun reading this paper as I had swimming with the dolphins.

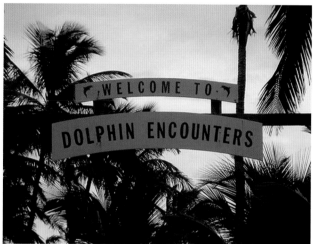

Now it's time to learn about dolphins. First, their diet consists of herring, mackerel, mullet, or capelin, but that is only a few of the many things they eat. They eat shrimp and squid as well.

Second, you do not want to go searching inside of a dolphin's mouth because inside their mouths are about 88 to 120 reasons to keep your hands out. So if you do not want a trim then I would stay out of there.

Because of humans, the dolphins have a hard life. People are polluting the waters that dolphins live in which could make dolphins extinct. So could you please help stop pollution in the sea? It will help more than just the dolphins live long healthy lives in the sea. Dolphin Encounters is one of the many places helping the dolphins. When they take in a dolphin they commit to training and help the dolphins so they will be healthy and live a long time.

Now I will talk about the fins of the dolphin. First, the fin on the top of the dolphin is used as a keel on a boat. The fin on the tail of the dolphin is used to propel the dolphin through the water at speeds of up to 25 miles per hour.

If you were wondering about the dolphin's sight underwater, they have a jelly like layer over their eye which keeps the salt and irritation out of their eyes. You know how your eye gets stung if salt water gets into it? If the dolphin did not have this layer, their eyes would get stung from the salt water as well.

Did you know that the dolphin does not have a sense of smell, but it does have an excellent sense of hearing? Dolphins are like a bats, which have built in sonar that can detect an object and scan an object and determine the length and size and how far away an object is.

Did you ever think about the way a dolphins travel? They travel in social groups. There are three kinds of groups; adult males, juvenile males, and the mothers and young females. The female will pick the most successful male in the group for a mate.

If you were wondering about joining the Dolphin Encounter here are some things you might want to consider before you do. First, what kind of a job do you want to do, animal training, education, research, veterinary care, conservation groups, or wildlife studies? But that is only a few of the many opportunities for you. Next, what kind of education is needed? You will need a college degree or formal education. Third, experience. You will need to have some experience with animals. If you don't have experience, but live near a beach call your local Coast Guard to join.

I will now talk about a kind of dolphin called the Bottle Nose Dolphin. It lives in the Atlantic Ocean. Now dolphins are all different in size, length, and how they act. If you want the biggest dolphin, go to the United Kingdom where the dolphins weigh up to 1,200 pounds and have a length of fourteen feet. If you look in the shallow waters of the Bahamas, the dolphins only grow to nine feet and weight 500 pounds. In the wild the dolphins only live thirty years at most because of pollution, predators, and food shortages. The oldest dolphin in captivity is fifty four years old. There used to be 100 deaths of dolphins each year; now there are about 3,000 each season, which will soon make them extinct. But, I hope that they live long and don't become extinct.

Now it's time to have some fun! When I did the dolphin swim, first they had the dolphins do jumps and then we went into the water and we petted them. Then they did the human hurdle where they jump over you, which was neat. Then we did the "foot push" where they push you by your foot with their nose. I got the longest ride and I couldn't even see where I was going.

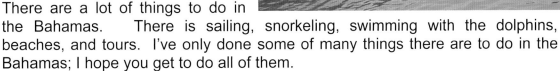

The Dolphin Encounter was a great way to learn about the dolphins, how they live, the problems they deal with, and to actually interact with them face-to-face. I gained much more knowledge and respect for these beautiful creatures.

There are a lot of things to do in the Bahamas. There is sailing, snorkeling, swimming with the dolphins, beaches, and tours. I've only done some of many things there are to do in the Bahamas; I hope you get to do all of them.

Elvis and Graceland

February 6, 2003

I would like to tell you about Elvis and his home, Graceland I learned about his family, his home, his music and hobbies.

When Elvis was born his family was very poor and lived in Tupelo, Mississippi. Elvis' family member's names were Gladys, his mom, Vernon, his dad, Jessie, his uncle, and Minnie, Elvis' grandmother. Elvis was born Jan 8, 1935.One year after Elvis and his twin brother, Jesse Garon, were born

Dr. William R. Hunt signed Elvis and Jesse's birth certificate. In 1948 the Presley family moved to Memphis, Tennessee.

A doctor built Graceland in 1936; the home was twenty-one years old when Elvis bought Graceland in 1957 for $102,500. Fifteen days after Elvis bought Graceland Elvis was accused of pulling a gun on Hershel Nixon, a young Marine, in downtown Memphis across from the Hotel Chisca. Nixon claimed that Elvis insulted his wife. The gun turned out to be a fake gun.

Elvis music was influenced by gospel and blues which he blended into his own brand of rock 'n' roll. Elvis became known as the king of rock 'n' roll. Elvis bought his first guitar in 1946; it cost $7.91. Elvis first performance was at a talent show in Tupelo where he won 2nd place. Elvis' music was the first of it's kind.

Elvis had 140 gold and platinum records; he had 75 gold and 65 platinum albums. He had more gold albums because it takes 500,000 records sold for gold and 1,000,000 records sold for platinum, so it was a lot easier to get gold. Elvis had thirty-one movies that were released including Blue Hawaii, Paradise Hawaiian Style, and Girls, Girls, Girls.

I read on a sign at Graceland that Elvis would always let people back stage for autographs and to make comments to him. He would always listen to his fans and he would always treat others with kindness and respect and hoped others would do the same.

Elvis's wife Pricilla was born in New York on May 24, 1945. She is an actress; she was twenty-one when she married Elvis.

Elvis's daughter Lisa Marie was born in Memphis on February 01, 1968. She has become a singer, just like her dad was.

Elvis' mother and father died at the ages of 46 and 63. His mother died in 1958, the same year Elvis when into the Army. Elvis died at the age of 42 in 1977 and he was buried at Graceland near his mother and father. They now rest in peace for eternity for all to memorialize this wonderful man who changed the direction of music for generations to come.

Elvis had a huge impact on the music we listen to today. He truly was the "King of Rock and Roll" and his music will live on forever.

Alaska
July 17, 2003

The history of Alaska started back in 1741 when Peter The Great sent Vitus Bering of Russia to explore the north Pacific. Russia used Alaska for its fur, gold and mining. At one point Russia told the United States that America companies could no longer operate in Alaska. On March 30, 1867, Secretary of State, William H. Seward, bought Alaska from the Russian for $7.2 million, or two cents per acre. The purchase of Alaska was often called Seward's folly or Seward's icebox. Alaska has two holidays named after it's purchase Seward's Day and Alaska Day.

Alaska became a state on Jan 3, 1959. Russia was willing to sell Alaska to the United States because of their defeat in the Crimean war and America was willing to buy Alaska to maintain sole dominance in North America.

The population of Alaska is currently 626,932 and Alaska's capital is Juneau. Alaska is on the Pacific Ocean and it has 33,904 miles of shoreline, more than any other state. Alaska has one of the largest glacier concentrations in the world; estimated at 100,000 glaciers. The glaciers form on mountains and plateaus; there are some glaciers that form at the base of mountains and plateaus. Alaska is the biggest state in the United States.

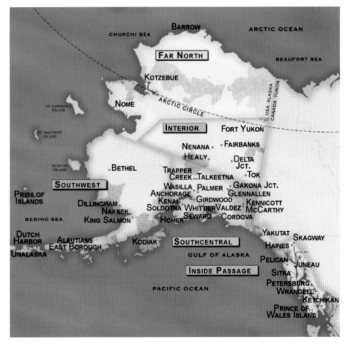

The main fish of Alaska are salmon, and halibut. King salmon average between forty and sixty pounds and the largest ever caught was ninety-seven pounds on the Kenai River. The average halibut weighs fifty pounds; the largest halibut caught was 459 pounds out of Dutch Harbor, Alaska.

There are fifteen different types of whales in Alaska; the most common is the humpback.

The food of Alaska is mainly fish. I have tried halibut and sockeye. I like the halibut better, but I don't care for garlic on it because it overwhelms the fish if you put too much on it. I hope you get a chance to try halibut and I hope you like it.

The fishing in Alaska is mainly king salmon, sockeye salmon, halibut, and silver salmon. I have gone halibut, king salmon, and red salmon (sockeye) fishing. The limit for king salmon is one per day and a limit of two per year per person. The limit on sockeye is three per day. I went sockeye fishing for one day and I caught three fish, which is about fifteen pounds of sockeye. The halibut limit is two per day per person. I went halibut fishing for two days and caught about 120 pounds of fish. The limit for silver salmon is fifteen per day depending on where you go. I did not go fishing for silvers. I was told that it is a lot of fun and they are jumping out of the water in to the boat. Silver salmon are only about five to

ten pounds. I caught a 57 lb halibut by putting a two pound weight on my line and bobbing it on the ocean bottom. The bait is herring and octopus. I went out to the Cook Inlet for my halibut. I saw sea otters on our way out to the fishing area.

I went King salmon fishing out on the Kenai River. I caught a forty three pound king salmon by letting the river current pull the bait through the water. Salmon eggs and quick fish were used as bait.

We flew on a float plane to a remote lake to go sockeye salmon fishing. I don't know how big my sockeye salmon were, but they are usually about five to ten pounds each.

You catch sockeye salmon by snagging them with lures. There were so many sockeye that you simply cast your lure into the area the fish are in and "hook" or "snag" them. However, you must snag them in the mouth for it to be a legal catch.

When we went fishing for sockeye salmon there where five bears also fishing there; a mother bear, a grown bear cub, which still nursed off of the mother bear, and 3 smaller cubs. The mother bear would dive off of a rock to catch her fish.

My dad got to play tug-of-war with one of the bear cubs. This happened when the bear cub started to pull the anchor rope so my dad started to pull back.

I had a great time learning about the history, geography, food, fish, and fishing of Alaska.

Schooling And Banking Of The Bahamas

December 16, 2003

I got to travel to Nassau, Bahamas, again for three weeks. I would like to tell you what I learned during this trip about the schooling and the banking of the Bahamas. In schooling this will consist of what, how, religion, and activities that the school taught at that time that I went to a Bahamian school. In banking, this will consist of who manages the money, functions, and how my father is helping to change things at the Central Bank of The Bahamas.

The first part of this story will be about what my teacher taught me while I was in the Bahamas. I got a chance to attend a school in the Bahamas for three weeks in December 2003. The school was the Christian Heritage School (CHS). All of the kids at the school wear a uniform. I also got to wear a uniform during the time I attended the school.

I was told that I had just missed exams and that I was lucky. I was put into the fifth grade and was supposed to be put into sixth grade, but the teacher was sick and I said I wanted be with the friends I already had. My teacher was Mrs. Culmer. She was very nice about things. The principal's name is Mrs. Harrison. She was extremely nice about things as well, in fact she even loaned me some money when my father forgot to give me money for lunch. I ended up paying back the money the next day for lunch.

My teacher normally taught math, science, Bible lessons, creative writing, and P.E or physical endurance, but not all on the same day. Normally she would have it spread out over each week. P.E is when the class races to the end of a field that is 500-feet long and back. Then we play freeze tag, boys against girls, but that's only on Friday. The religion that my school taught is Christianity, which is when you strongly believe in God and Jesus Christ. That is why they study the Bible.

I got to enjoy the wonders of the school named Christian Heritage School. It is not very big, but more of a family school. It has two buildings that make up the school. One has the principal's office, computer room, and the sixth grade class.

I also got to be in a Christmas Music Festival on the 13th December 2003. I sang

the song "Deck The Halls". It was very fun and I got to watch other people sing as well.

You know how we use computers a lot here in the United States? They don't use them in the Bahamas. I have only seen a computer once this entire trip at the school, so they use paper a lot for math, writing, and even for computer class.

The second part of this paper will explain things about The Central Bank of The Bahamas. First thing is who manages The Central Bank of The Bahamas? This would start with the Governor, Mr. Francis. He is the head of the whole Bank. He oversees all parts of the Central Bank. I haven't gotten a chance to meet Mr. Francis yet.

Then there is the Deputy Governor, Mrs. Craigg. My father knows her very well. He goes out to dinner with her every once in awhile. I see her almost every day I am in the Bahamas. She only has one person who tells her what to do, that is the Governor. She tells the Governor what is going on in the Bank.

Next are the functions that The Central Bank of The Bahamas performs. One - Regulation of the money supply. This requires money deposits from other banks. Two – The Banker's bank. This requires free deposits from other banks. Three - Adviser to the Minister of Finance. This means that the Bank reports to the Minister of Finance.

The Central Bank of The Bahamas manages and oversees all of the other three hundred and fifty banks in the Bahamas. This is called the Bank Supervision Department. The Bank also controls all money coming in or going out of the country. This is called the Exchange Control Department. You must get permission to bring large amounts of money into the Bahamas or to take large amounts of money out of the Bahamas.

My father is helping to change things a lot at the Bank. They used to use paper for every thing now my father is taking all that and putting it into a computer system that will be easier and faster way to document the processes at The Bank. My father said he would show me a room where the whole room is filled with papers from the Bank all that could be put in to anywhere from three to five computers. So my father is helping to change the Bank into an easier place for people to work.

I hope that you learned something about the schooling and banking of the Bahamas because I sure did.

Homestead Crater Diving

May 11, 2004

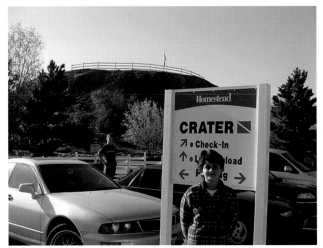

My Mom, Dad, and I went to the Homestead Crater, located just east of Salt Lake City, to complete our "open-water dives" and become scuba certified divers.

We found that the crater was a perfect place to become certified because the water was 93 degrees and the air is 60 degrees. The crater stays warm because of the circulating water of a spring under the crater (see diagram). The spring was created 10,000 years ago by water seeping through a crack as far down as 3250 feet. As the water went farther down into the earth it picked up additional carbon dioxide. As the water boiled up to the surface it dissolved a limestone crater. When the water broke the surface the carbon dioxide disappeared into the air and the water stopped dissolving the limestone. The history of the crater goes back to the mining days in the early 1900's. It was used for miners to relax because of the hot water and mineral water.

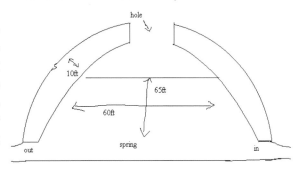

My experience in the Homestead Crater was excellent. There were no distractions during our diving, such as fish or plants, and the water was very warm. We all got open water certified and were very happy.

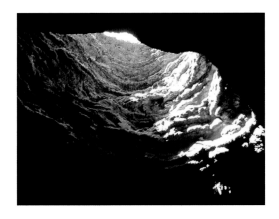

After our first day of diving we went to the Sundance Resort. We had dinner with all of the people that we scuba dived with. The resort is owned by the actor, Robert Redford. The Sundance Resort, which is 30 minutes away from the Homestead Crater, has a hotel, restaurants, ski lifts and ski runs, swimming pool, river, spa, and shops. It is a non-profit organization for the arts. The Sundance Film Festival, a famous event to help promote new film makers, is held every January at the Sundance Resort.

Now that I am a certified scuba diver I am looking forward to many more scuba diving adventures with my family.

Grand Canyon
June 13, 2004

Imagine a crack in the ground. Imagine this crack being 277 river miles long, 18 miles across in some places, and 8,100 ft tall at its highest point from river to rim. Now imagine the erosion of water and volcanoes meeting under ground - water, fire, ice, and wind eroding away the ground over hundreds of millions of years; the continental plate slowly moving northwest.

If you can imagine this you have imagined the creation of the Grand Canyon, because all this happened and more. It is because of these natural forces occurring as they did, which created the Grand Canyon. I (for one) appreciate what we were blessed with.

On my second trip to the northern part of Arizona I saw a great wonder and beauty. I believe its wonder can never be matched and its beauty will always be recognized. This is the GRAND CANYON!!!

The first inhabitants of the Grand Canyon were Indians who lived from 2000 B.C till today. The Grand Canyon is surrounded by several major Indian reservations. The largest reservation is the Navajo encompassing 17.5 million acres.

You know when you stumble across something important, but you don't tell anyone? Then someone else gets credit for finding it? This is how Francisco Vasquez De Coronado might have felt in 1540 because he was the first person to discover the Grand Canyon, but he didn't tell his government. The Americans got credit for finding the canyon. The second person to discover the Grand Canyon was Major John Wesley Powell. He and nine other explorers set out on the most exciting adventure. Only five emerged from the canyon. The other five people either died when they lost a boat or were killed by Indians.

Major Powell was always adventurous and wanted excitement. Lake Powell, located in southern Utah, was named after him. Amazingly, John Powell only had one arm; he lost his arm during the civil war. In 1869 he conquered the canyon's river and rapids. He was the first to map the river. Powell and his men emerged at the mouth of the Colorado River with a map in hand. He then made a second voyage down the canyon in 1871-72.

The canyon name was put in place in 1869 when John Powell nicknamed it the Grand Canyon.

Miners, traders, and trailblazers prospered in the canyon during the 1870's. There were only two places to cross the canyon (by ferry) Lee's ferry in 1871 and Pierce ferry in 1876.

There are three dams that affect the Grand Canyon; Hoover Dam, Glen Canyon Dam, and Marble Canyon Dam. Glen Canyon Dam and Marble Canyon Dam are north of the Grand Canyon which affects the flow of the water going into the Canyon. Hoover Dam is south of the Grand Canyon and affects the flow out of the Canyon. These dams have a bad effect on wild life like fish, but it also has a plus on the plant life because plants have a chance to reseed instead of being washed away by flash floods.

The Grand Canyon became a national park in 1919 because it is recognized as one of the natural wonders of the world and it needs protection. I believe that the

Canyon should be protected a lot more than it is. There are a lot of ranger services and tours, but if you want a mule ride you will have to plan it up to eight months ahead of time.

I had a great experience at the Grand Canyon because I saw many wonders. I realized I love it and saw that this is a great place because it is so peaceful.

I believe the Grand Canyon is of great importance to all that see it. It makes you know that you are not the biggest and best person or thing in the world. Those good things come in time and patience. I believe that we can all learn from the Grand Canyon. The wonder and beauty of the Grand Canyon is amazing anyway you see it.

Meteor Crater

June 14, 2004

Have you ever thought what would happen if a 50 meter asteroid were hurling towards Earth at eleven miles per second? I witnessed the result of this awesome feat. The answer is Meteor Crater located thirty-five miles east of Flagstaff, Arizona just off Highway 40.

Over 50,000 years ago an asteroid half the size of a football field in diameter hit the Earth's surface going eleven miles per second, meaning it would take approximately five minutes to get from Paris to New York and only three minutes to get from New York to Arizona. Within ten seconds Meteor Crater was formed. It was seventy stories deep and almost one mile long. During its creation within a radius of a few miles several hundred million tons of rock was blown over the landscape. Rocks were blown onto their sides and boulders, the size of small houses, were blown miles away, followed by hurricane winds that blew top soil away to uncover flagstone. Earthquakes made the land waiver up and down, making everything rough and rocky, while everything only a few miles away was undisturbed.

Meteor Crater is the first proven and best-preserved meteorite crater on Earth. In the 1800's there was a big dispute over whether the crater was formed by a meteor or a volcano. In 1891 G. K. Gillbert briefly visited the crater and said a volcano created it. In 1903 Daniel Moreau Barringer found iron in the soil so he bought the mineral rights and drilled to a depth of 1,376 feet. The drill finally stopped when it hit a large meteor fragment

and was stuck for good. Barringer drilled for 26 years. Before he died in 1929, he saw the science community agree that a meteor created Meteor Crater. This was a major accomplishment for Mr. Barringer.

Today the crater is the same width as when it was created, but now the depth is only equal to a sixty story building because of wind and storms. The land is currently leased to Bar T Bar until 2154. In 1964 to 1972 the crater was used for astronaut training. There are platforms for overlooking the crater.

The meteor that created the crater was an iron/nickel meteor and severely "shocked", meaning it was compressed on impact and very rough. There are three types of "shocked" rocks, which are rocks found on Earth and in space; non-shocked rocks, which are not very, rough and are basically the rocks you find in your back yard; mildly shocked, which are rocks that you find on the moon and are sort of rough; and severely shocked, which are rocks you would find in a crater and are very rough.

Today scientists are very concerned that a meteor may hit the Earth so they keep a close watch on asteroid activity and are prepared to defend the Earth from destruction. One of the things they do is have astronauts map asteroids that are near Earth. Some asteroids, comets, and iron meteors can destroy the Earth. Based upon some experiments I made on a console at Meteor Crater, I have determined that an iron/nickel meteor only 180 km (112 miles) in diameter would be sufficient to destroy the Earth.

The iron/nickel asteroid that made Meteor Crater was about twice as heavy as sandstone the same size from Earth. This is because of the density of the iron meteor. A crater made by a meteor is very similar to a crater made by a nuclear test.

I think Meteor Crater is a wonderful place to visit. It is very educational for children and adults. I loved the crater and the museum. Don't worry; a meteor big enough to destroy the Earth is not coming …. YET!

Petrified Forest
June 14, 2004

Let's go back six million years, back to when dinosaurs first roamed the Earth, but this isn't the topic of the story. This is a story about wood...petrified wood, that is, located in eastern Arizona.

The Petrified Forest was formed 4-8 million years ago by a river going through a single continent. This is when all the continents were one and North America was sub-tropical with ferns, itopsidemas (similar to palms), and of course trees of many shapes and sizes. Over time the river widened and eroded the rock away until the trees fell to their destiny in the river. The river narrowed and the trees jammed in the river. Water logged, the trees sank to the bottom of the river. The river started to deposit silica onto the logs, which started to either completely replace the wood cells with mineral deposits or encase the cells of the wood; this is why there are some kinds of petrified wood that look like wood and some that look like rock.

Over millions of years the Earth's movement and erosion moved the logs higher and higher until they were visible to the world. After thousands of years of being visible miners came and found semi-precious gems in the Petrified Forest. A railroad went in and a town (Adamana) sprang up. People started taking petrified wood. The people of Adamana hated this. They tried to get the President of the United States to make the land a federal park, and it wasn't until President Theodore Roosevelt made it the nation's second national monument that people stopped taking petrified wood, and even then some people dared to take some but very few did or do.

Before modern people came to the forest there were Indians who had adapted to life in the desert with a calendar to tell them when to plant crops. They also had hieroglyphics that they wrote on rocks and boulders. The cities they had were normally near water and housed about 200 people.

Today the Petrified Forest is very nice with a lot of trails to hike and many logs to see. My experience was wonderful. I got to see the world's largest petrified log it was about nine feet in diameter and thirty feet long. The world's longest log is one hundred and fifty feet long and three feet in diameter.

If you are a child you can also become a Junior Park Ranger and help protect our nation's national parks. It is a very simple process. You have to fill out a workbook that asks you to find things throughout the park, answer questions about animals and plants in the park, and draw pictures and diagrams of various things. Once you have completed the workbook, you get "sworn-in" as a Junior Park Ranger by a qualified Park Ranger. Myself and my two sisters all became Junior Park Rangers at the Petrified Forest and received our Junior Park Ranger badges.

The Petrified Forest is still being made today because some logs are not uncovered. You may even have petrified wood in you own back yard, because all countries and all of the States in the USA have petrified wood.

Cancun and The Mayan Culture
July 5, 2004

Part One – Pre-Visit Research

If you go to the city of Cancun, Mexico today you will see many resorts and people having fun, but this is not our destination. Let's go farther back – 300 years before Christ – to where the Mayans lived. There will be much peril, but do not fear. The Mayans will survive, but, oh, not many – only about 6 million of them.

There are three periods in the Mayan history the pre-classic (2500 B.C-250 A.D), classic (250 A.D-1000 A.D), and post-classic (1000 A.D-1500 A.D) periods. In the pre-classic period the Mayans based many of their inventions on earlier cultures, such as the Olmecs. In this period people got together and decided to leave the Olmecs around 300 B.C, and they found space in the southern lowlands.

In the classic period, the southern region cities, Tikal, Uaxactun, Caracol, Copan, Yaxchilan, Pidras, Negras, Calkmal, and Palenque, fell to ruin. There were many thoughts on why these cities collapsed; over-growth, warfare, and natural disaster are some of the considerations.

The post-classic began when the Mayans immigrated to the Yucatan peninsula. These ruins, south of Cancun are definitely worth a visit. The Mayans lived in relative peace around 1000 A.D-1100 A.D. After 1100 A.D the Mayan rival cities would compete for land and power until the Spaniards invaded the land in the 1500's. The Spaniards brought a disease (Matlalzahuatl), which devastated the Mayan culture. The Mexican people from other parts of the country invaded the Mayan lands, finding it easy to overthrow the vulnerable Mayans. The Mexican people burnt every Mayan book and scroll, but fortunately three survived.

The Popul Vuh is considered part of the bible to the Mayans. In 1558 in was written in the Quiche language. Around 1758 it was found in Chichicastenango, Guatemala. Around 1858 it was put on display at the Newberry Library in Chicago where it is today. The Mayan religion consisted of human and blood letting sacrifice, deities (gods), and She Bal Bah (Underworld). When their people die they were believed to go to Xibalba (She Bal Bah) where gods would trick the visitors. These religions define if a population is Mayan or not.

The Mayan diets varied by location, but the main diet was maize (cornmeal) cooked as flat bread with beans, squash, and chili peppers.

The Mayans invented many things that are still in use today. The Maya had a complex hieroglyphics system with many symbols. The Maya invented the zero in math. They also only used three symbols to make numbers; a shell (0), a dot (1), and a bar (5). They were extremely good at mathematics as well. They were known for their architecture without metal tools. They invented the corbel arch, a type of architecture is still used today. They invented a calendar that took 52 years to complete a cycle; this cycle will be over in 8 years.

The Mayan's played a ball game was mainly used to symbolize seasons, planting, or harvesting. In the game the winning captain would present his head to the losing captain and the loser would decapitate the winner (not real motivating for the winner, if you ask me). This was supposedly the ultimate prize because the winner goes to heaven straight away instead of going through the thirteen believed steps to get to heaven. The game was played on a field with two variations, "hand ball" or "big ball". The padding used in this game was a half mask, chin guard, elbow pads, kneepads, waist pads, leather apron, and a palmate stone. You were not allowed to use your hands, feet, or calves to touch the ball. In some cases the loser would be decapitated. The name of this game is Pok-A-Tok. Sometimes prisoners would be sent to play the ball game as gladiators in final combat. Reconstruction has been started on one of the ball courts in Chichen Itza; the reason for picking this court over the other twenty-two is because it is the largest of them. In the ball court a whisper can be heard from the other end of the court and is getting clearer as construction proceeds.

The Mayans endured many perils, but they strived to help their culture survive and their legacy lives on in the hearts of the Mayan today. I believe that the most important part of the Mayan culture is they were able to endure the hard ships and still survived.

Part Two – My Observations

I have told you what happened 2300 years ago, but what you haven't heard is probably the most important part of the Maya history… Chichen Itza.

On my recent trip with my mom, dad, and two sisters, to the Mayan ruins of Chichen Itza, I discovered more about the Mayan culture. I got to climb the Mayan temple, which was very steep, with my dad and my sister, Samantha. I also saw the inside of the temple. The ruins were very hot and humid. I enjoyed this trip a lot thanks to my mother and father.

This is one of many cities the Maya built in the southern Yucatan peninsula. In Chichen Itza there are two cities – the old city and the new city, Ortec. The old city was strictly built by Mayans in the early classic period (250 A.D-1000 A.D). In the late post-classic period (1000A.D-1500A.D) the Ortec influence generated a newer version of architecture and culture.

The architecture of the Mayans is very complex. There are carvings of the gods and paintings of warriors. The gods were used in everything (stairs, walls, ceilings, and corners). It was interesting to see this because it made every thing have a sense of importance.

The Mayan religion was reflected in all their buildings, carvings, and architecture. The Mayans believed the gods brought good luck so they were used in all their art form. On stairs and handrails snakes were often used. Two entwining snakes, one going up and one going down, with holes carved in the stair rail making it seem life like. These snakes symbolize the fertility god. In the old city, rain gods were used regularly on corners and over doors. These gods are human looking until you get closer and you see a long spiraling nose like an elephant. The wind gods (human head and wings of an eagle) help the rain gods. They live in a center island in front of the temple.

The jaguar symbolizes the total Mayan culture or death. It is only carved in one structure (the sacrifice platform). The jaguar is holding a heart (or sacrifice) to the gods. The eagle is the Ortec culture, which is also holding a heart. The one other god used in carving was a skull, which symbolized human sacrifice. There are three steps to this ritual; one decapitation, which would take place at one of the three platforms. There are slanted pillars the sacrifice would lean against. The second step they would put the head on a stake for the whole city to see and admire. The third step to take the body to the last platform where the priest (ruler) would take the heart out and eat it.

It was believed that thirteen branches would sprout from the body and nine branches would sprout from the head. The body representing the thirteen levels of heaven and the head represents the nine under world kingdoms. One of these would light up which would be the kingdom or heaven the person would end up at.

The Mayan had a complex way of telling time. Most of the houses had a crack in the ceiling. The light would show down on the ground. They had rocks on the ground to indicate the hours. They used a stick to plug the crack when it rained. Their complete calendar consisted of three calendars the sun, month, and year. This took a total of fifty-two years to complete a cycle. This would go around like a dartboard with one circle inside the other, which would coincide with the other to make a day, month, or year. The Mayans believed that human history has distinct periods (or "suns") of 3,000 - 5,000 years, after which there is a catastrophic event that completely ends all existing civilizations. The Mayan start date of our era is similar to the start date for the Egyptian civilization, according to modern archaeologists. According to the Mayans the present era began on 13 August 3114 B.C. and will end on 21 December 2012 A.D. (I hope there were wrong – I will only be nineteen years old).

The houses of the Maya all used corbel arches. The roofs were made with rock and cement which would be held in place with sticks but these have long since disintegrated. These houses did not seem very big, but they held up to thirty occupants, because they stack beds on top of each other like bunk beds.

The population of the cities in Chichen Itza was about 6,000 inside and 3,000 living outside the cities.

The Ortecs were a later civilization that came from the Aztecs in the later post-classic period. These people built over the buildings that the Mayans had started constructing. You can see the architectural difference between the two cities.

The paintings on the walls were mainly of warriors in battle with spears and  arrows that were vibrant with red, green, yellow, blue, and black colors. The outer layer of stucco and paint was lost in time.

The Mayan astronomy was one of their most important aspects. They were able to track four of the nine planets (Mars, Venus, Saturn, and Earth); this helped them to tell time. They believed the planets were stars.

The ball court of Chichen Itza was a huge stadium with hoops thirty feet off the ground. People would have to hit a five-pound ball (without hands, or feet) into these hoops. It is believed that the hoop represents the sun and the ball was the earth revolving around the sun.

The great temple was built by Maya and Ortec. Eighteen temples were stacked on top of each other with 365 steps, which somehow these two numbers adds up to 52. This temple is hard to explain in words so I supplied a picture.

In March and September the lights and the shadows happens. It seems that the snake slithers down the stair rail. This is because the shadows created by the sun on the corners of the temple making the snake appear to slither down.

I have told you what was, but there are other stories to tell about how the Mayans live on (six million people). Their legacy is not over, but those stories will have to wait for another time.

Alaska

September 3,2004

My second trip to Alaska started on August 21, 2004, and it was a long day. We left Colorado at 5:00 PM and arrived in Anchorage, Alaska at 8:00 PM. We got to stay at the Hilton Garden Inn in Anchorage. The next day my family (Samantha, Stephanie, mom, dad, grandma, and I) drove to the Soldotna Silver Tip Lodge in the town of Soldotna and unpacked. The next day we all got up at 4:00 AM to go "butt" (halibut) fishing. All six of us went fishing. The limit for halibut fish was two fish per person per day, plus four extra for the captain and first mate. Our family caught a total of 475 lbs of fish, a record for that boat that year. Three of our fish were over 50 lbs.; one 52 lbs, one 60 lbs, and one was whopping a **92 lbs!!!** That monster was caught by my sister Samantha. We also caught silver salmon and black bass, which are very beautiful.

While catching silvers we watched what our captain said was "a two ton humpback whale" feed off of plankton. This whale was wonderful to watch. The captain of our boat was Captain Rick. He was a great captain. His first mate was "THE OLD" (his real name was Bill). He was called "Old" because he always worked with younger people and the name stuck. When we got back to the dock and cleaned the fish, they took the ear bones out of the 92-pound halibut and made earrings as a birthday present for Samantha.

The next day we all had to get up at 4:00 AM again and to go silver salmon fishing. We had to go in two boats my dad, Stephanie, and I in one boat and my mom, grandma, and Samantha in the other. It was boys vs. girls; Stephanie was made an honorary boy for the day. Stephanie even tinkled in the can and had a great time. We all caught two silver salmon each, but the girls won by getting all their fish first. We went silver salmon fishing three other times. The last day we went fishing we saw a moose and her baby. Right when we got to the cabin we saw another moose with her twins.

Samantha and Dad's birthday was during this trip. Samantha got a necklace, two cakes, halibut earrings, bracelet, and an Eskimo doll. My Dad got a letter opener, wine stopper, pen and holder, and an Alaska picture frame. During our stay in Anchorage we went to the Alaska State Fair and saw chickens, llamas, sheep, rabbit, turkey, horse, cows, and much more. I won a stuffed animal on a game where you try to get a ball in a barrel, but the ball doesn't stay in easily. Samantha and I rode an

octopus ride, which I hated because we were the first ones on and I was sitting at the top of the ride forever.

I believe this trip was fantastic. We all had fun especially when we went to the movies where we watched Hero, which was in Chinese. After ten days in Alaska we left Anchorage at 11:30 PM and got back to Colorado at 7:30 AM.

Puerto Vallarta

September 28, 2004

I once visited a city, a very old city, but it was nice in its own way. This city and my experiences I would like to share with you. The city is Puerto Vallarta.

At the airport, when leaving for Mexico, my mother forgot to grab her and my passports. She had left them at home. She had forgotten that Mexico was another country. We had to go through some other process to get into Mexico.

At the Mexico airport foreign passengers have to go through a section where travel agents talk to you and try to sell you memberships when you are walking out of the airport. The police gave an agent a ticket for not stopping when my dad told them to "stop".

The time-share we stayed at was called Los Tules. It is the oldest time-share in Puerto Vallarta (thirty years old). Our room was right on the beach and 100 yards from the pool. It had three bedrooms, three bathrooms, full kitchen, dining room, living room, and two patios. My dad and I thought it looked old, but was a nice hotel.

We (my mom, dad, and I) went diving in Puerto Vallarta because it is good diving. We went out with Chico's Dive Shop. We went diving in four different places. The first dive was at Los Arcos. This was a shallow dive at thirty-five feet. Our second dive was seventy-eight feet. We went on a catamaran and saw turtles from the boat. These turtles were coming into shore to lay their eggs. During the dive we saw eels, starfish, puffer fish, and

all kinds of tropical fish. Each of our two dives were about 45 minutes each. After the second dive my mom came up and got sick.

Our second day of diving was at a place more than one hour from shore. The dive site called El Morro. This is supposedly where the big fish are. We went out on a smaller speedboat. On the first dive my dad was the first in and forgot to inflate his BCD, buoyancy compensation device – the inflatable vest you wear when diving, and started sinking. You are supposed to inflate your BCD before you jump in. From the boat we saw tarpon and other fish jumping out of the water. We also saw some turtles. Our dives were 45 minutes with a maximum depth of 93 ft, my deepest dive ever!!! During the dive we saw tarpon, puffer fish, eels, lobster, and a turtle.

On our third day of diving some friends joined us in Puerto Vallarta and stayed with us. Their names are Cesar, Anna, and their two children Sophie (3 years old), and Santiago (7 months old). This was their first dive ever. Cesar went first and he had a lot of fun. He held a puffer fish and saw a dead moray eel. Next, Anna dived and she held a starfish, sea anemone, sea urchins, and saw plenty of things she had never seen before. Each of their dives was about 45  minutes. The fourth place we dived was a place called Majahuits and the diving was pretty bad. We could only see ten feet ahead of us because of the recent rains and run-off into the ocean; luckily it was a shallow dive and we stayed down for about 56 minutes. After lunch instead of going back to that dive site we went back to Los Arcos for our second dive. Cesar and his family went on these dives as well. Our last dive was to Marietta's, which is right near El Morro. We saw many types of fish, eels, and sea creatures.

Puerto Vallarta is a large town that sits on a bay and my dad said it reminded him of his hometown of Santa Cruz, California where he grew up, with cobble streets, old buildings, and the sense of easy going. Puerto Vallarta is a wonderful town.

Leaving Mexico was a lot easier than getting in because we had authorization in Denver. We only had to show photo ID. My diver certification card came in handy because it identified me with my picture on it. On the way home from the airport with my mom, dad, grandmother, and sisters, I told them all about our trip, basically every thing I have said in this paper.

I hope you had a good time with me diving in Puerto Vallarta, because I sure did!

Ecuador
February 12-March 02, 2005

Galapagos Islands

The Galapagos Islands are a strange and mysterious place. There are things that you will find nowhere else in the world, but strangely enough the islands characteristics are the same as other places in the world.

The Galapagos are oceanic islands, meaning that they were never connected to any landmass by a land bridge of any sort (this is the reason for the shortage of land animals). The islands range in age from 4 million to 700,000 years old. The oldest is Espanola and the youngest is Santiago. Volcanoes created the islands. The earth's surface is broken into seven large and many small moving plates. These plates, each about fifty miles thick, move an average of a few inches a year. The islands sit on a plate that is smaller than most plates; therefore the islands vary more widely in age than other volcanic islands. Unlike the magma in Hawaii, Galapagos lava is the "basic" type, whereas Hawaii is part "acid". The "basic" lava turns brown then brick red as the iron in it oxidizes.

The islands are located about 600 miles off the coast of Ecuador. The equator (middle of the earth) actually goes right across the Wolf volcano on Isabella Island. The islands are on a plate that is moving about six centimeters per year. This is the reason that the islands vary in age is because the "hot spots" stay in the same place, but the area that they erupt in does not.

Most of the plants and animals on Galapagos come from Ecuador. One way for the plants to get to the islands is wind. Most seeds will float on warm air currents in the sky. Another way is floatation in the ocean. Most seeds have a thin pocket of air between the skin and the nut making them float. Also, birds that eat seeds in Ecuador and travel to the Galapagos then leave their droppings. Animals were able to ride on small natural rafts or float there. Once there they must adapt to a diet of mostly sea vegetation.

Fray Tomas de Berlanga, the bishop of Panama, first discovered the Galapagos in 1535. Berlanga was not an explorer and found the islands by accident. He was sailing to Peru when he got caught in a strong current that pulled him to the islands. Here is what he said about the islands, "dross, worthless, because they do the power to grow a little grass, but only thistles". Berlanga named the islands "Insulae de los Galapagos" for the giant saddleback turtles they found. The Galapagos Islands were a great place for pirates to hide their treasure. By 1790 the pirates were replaced by whalers, which killed the tortoises for their main food, and many species became extinct. Another thing that the whalers killed were the fur sea lions whose fur was and still is highly prized among the Spanish empire.

The natives of the islands were people who came from the mother country of Ecuador on small rafts that only held about 30 people. When they arrived they found little food because the animals that were introduced to the islands by pirates, such as goats, cats, and dogs, either ate the animals (dogs and cats ate the iguanas) or ate the food of the animals (goats ate the grass that the tortoises ate). Also whalers had killed as many as

200 tortoises in one day. Whalers killed off three of eleven species of tortoises

that lived in the Galapagos.

The habitat of the islands is harsh, with lava rocks as soil and little plant life. Only a few shrubs and trees grow there, but none of the beach palms you would regularly see on an island. There is little vegetation that the animals can eat so they have to adapt. The islands inhabitants are mammals, reptiles, birds, and marine life. Mammals are bats and sea lions. The reptiles include tortoises, such as the Giant Tortoise, Saddle Back Tortoise, and Dome Shaped Tortoise, turtles, iguanas, marine iguanas, and lava lizard. Birds are the most common animals in the Galapagos. There are the great frigates, blue footed boobies, red footed boobies, flamingos, short eared owls, penguins, barn owls, masked boobies, Galapagos hawks, and waved albatross (these are just a few of the different types of birds). You can only imagine how many different types of marine life there are in the Galapagos. There are dolphins, penguins, sharks, and almost every fish that you can think of swimming in the same water together.

Also, listed under tortoises is the Pinta Island Tortoise. Lonesome George is the soul survivor of this species. In 1972 he was moved from Pinta Island to the Darwin Research Facility on Santa Cruz Island and still resides there today. The reason for his species extinction was goats, in the 1800's. Through DNA research people are trying to find a mate for George.

Charles Darwin was the first person to discover that we came from something else before our race, that things change depending upon their home or environment. In 1835 he traveled the Galapagos in the small research boat "Beagle". He saw that there were twelve different types of finches and each one had something special to help it in its environment. In 1854 he published a book titled, "Origin of the Species". During that time it stirred up things in Spain about God not creating us, but the first day that his book came out it sold out! I believe Darwin's theories and think he was a great scientist. I also believe that God did create us. God created the things on earth that have then evolved over time.

I arrived in Quito Saturday Feb 12 and checked in to the Hilton Colon Quito and stayed there for one night. After that I went to the Galapagos Islands for five days. In the Galapagos we went to the Darwin Research Station where we saw Galapagos Giant Tortoises and Saddle Back Tortoises. Also at the research station there were Land Iguanas that we saw lying about or digging their burrows out. Our guide at that time got a cactus fruit, which is the iguanas' favorite food, and fed it to the Iguanas, but the second time he tried to get one he got badly barbed by the cactus.

In the Galapagos my dad, mom, and I went scuba diving (this was one of the main reasons we traveled to the Galapagos). The currents in the Galapagos are often impossible. There is a place called Gordon Rocks that is a very good dive site. It is a half circle of rocks and some days no matter where you are in that

semi circle you are against the current. At a place called Bartholomew, where we went scuba diving, at one point we were against the current, and then we were with the current; it kept switching through the entire dive.

My dad dove three times and I dove twice. We were planning on going three days (six dives), but I got sick the first day and the second day all of us had equipment problems so my mom and me didn't dive that day. The next day my dad and I went scuba diving, but my mom had problems again. The dives were very difficult and technical challenging due to the large water temperature changes, strong currents, and .large animals.

The Galapagos Islands is a place of wonder where almost anything can happen. You can see things that dazzle the mind and make you appreciate the world that we live. We often don't seem to appreciate the natural wonders all around us, but you become much more aware of in them in the Galapagos Islands and realized just how blessed we are in this world.

Quito, Ecuador

Quito seems like a place where the people are trying to better him or herself. Everyone is trying to help, and not only thinking of themselves. My mother, father and I felt very comfortable in this city.

After our stay in the Galapagos we stayed twelve days in Quito. The first day we went to a town called Otavalo were we spent the day looking at and buying souvenirs. We then went to Cotacachi and everyone got a new jacket. The day after we went to a market that was in a small square outside our hotel.

The city of Quito was first named Quitus after its Inca inhabitants, who in 1533 abandoned the city. General Ruminahui destroyed the city so that it would not fall into the hands of the conquistadors; nevertheless a year later the Spaniards conquered the Inca and took their land, so Quito was theirs. The city of Quito was captured (after two other voyages failed) in the early part of the 16th century. The conquerors took a path that had a lot of twists and turns. This road has been paved with cobblestones leading down the hillside into Quito. I was not able to finish traveling the road because of road construction.

After the Spanish conquered the Inca, a man named Sebastian De Benalcazar started to rebuild the city. Quito is actually two cities in one – the old city that shows the history of the city and the new city, which is more popular and buzzing with people and brand new buildings that tower over the area.

There is a town called Otavalo about one-hour drive from Quito and has a very large market that has mostly alpaca and hand-woven textiles. There are alpaca sweaters, rugs, blankets, scarves, capes, and even gloves. After we visited Otavalo we went to Cotacachi where the people are well known for their leather products. We saw belts, purses, jackets, hats, saddles, and other leather goods.

The markets in Ecuador are very cheap. In the States a small alpaca teddy bear would cost about $50 to $100, where as in Ecuador it cost $5 to $10. It is **ten times as much in the States!** That's insane!

Colonial Quito is the part of town that was built when the Spaniards moved to Quito. Most of the buildings are over three hundred years old! If you were to search the walls of the buildings you would find a lot of things that are worth a lot of money, such as religious artifacts and gold doubloons, which are gold coins. In fact, one of our guides said that they were going to tear down a building, and before they did the merchants came out with boxes of things that were worth thousands or even millions of dollars. These buildings are made of mud, stone, grass with a sand mortar, and a plaster made of crushed rock and water. The roofs are made of bamboo and palm leaves. Today the plaster is a basic type and some walls have been replaced or added, and the roofs are made of 2x4 lumber, screws, and tin.

My mother and father plan on making an investment in Quito. We looked at about ten houses for a bed and breakfast. So far we like the first one we looked at the best. It has a wonderful view of the Virgin statue, which is the city's main symbol and can be seen from all around the city. There is another place called the "castle" that we are told has a wonderful view as well, but it needs a lot of work because it was cracked bad, due to an earthquake, and it would take about $250,000 to repair; but it is a fantastic view of the plazas and the Virgin statue.

During my stay in Quito I met the person that sold us some property in the Galapagos Islands. His name is Andrés Córdova. He is an attorney in Quito. He regularly travels to the Galapagos Islands and is working on a project in the Galapagos called Ocean Hills. During the time that we were in Quito Andrés helped us in the process of buying the property in the Galapagos Islands. We had lunch at his house with Andrés and his wife Eliana, she is a very nice lady. The next day we had dinner at an oriental restaurant with  them. On Friday my father and I went to lunch with Eliana and went up to the Virgin (the symbol of Quito). By the way, did I mention that Andrés is the grandson of one of the presidents of Ecuador? His grandfather's name was Andrés F. Córdova and he was President of Ecuador from 1939-1940.

We also visited Papallacta, which are hot springs with pools that can get up to 110 degrees, with Andrés and Eliana Córdova. When the hot springs water first comes out of the ground it is up to 157 degrees. The hot springs are very natural and comfortable. They were made of lava rocks and sand mortar. The pools had a very natural feeling to it.

Quito was so peaceful and had the feeling of old, but not the oldness of mold and disgust. It was clean and marvelous. I loved the city and the people of Quito.

Carlsbad Caverns
August 5, 2005

During my trip this August to Carlsbad Caverns in Carlsbad, New Mexico, I had the feeling that I was a very small thing in this world. It was one of those things that I will never forget. You see the world is so large that you can't really tell that it is there or where it starts or stops. However, what if you could see the walls of the world around you? Carlsbad Caverns are huge, but you can still see the edge or the walls and it makes you feel small. It is a world of

its own, huge, but definable. Being able to see the boundaries give you a sense of how tiny we really are.

The history of the caverns dates back over 10,000 years when dinosaurs roamed the Earth. Animals came to the entrance of the caves and often fell into the depths of the deep hole. Normally, they would die in the twilight zone, the transition area from light to dark in the caves, because of the steep slope at the cave entrance. They would fall, hurt themselves and die or they would survive the fall, but couldn't find food and starve to death (personally, I would rather die quick, but that's just me). The first known human inhabitants of the caves were Native Americans around 250 B.C. They used the cave entrance for shelter. They would also use the caverns as a natural trap, but instead of the animal wandering in they would herd it in to the cave and let it die. Then they would go into the caves, bring the animal back up and they would eat it.

The second major inhabitants of the caverns were bats, Mexican Fee Tailed bats to be precise. No one knows how they got into the cave, but they were there. They found there way into the cave sometime around 300 A.D. The bats lived in peace until about 1898 when Jim White saw what he thought was a large, dark cloud in the distance. When he got closer he saw it was a swarm of bats. Later he went back with supplies to go down into the cave. He explored a little at a time and later he started conducting tours by taking other people in to the cave. The people touring the caverns treated Mr. White very nicely, because they knew that if anything happened to Mr. White they would be stuck down there forever since there weren't any paths to take them out. Back then a cave trip was an all day adventure because they didn't have the paths that you follow today. They climbed and crawled their way in and out of the caves.

In 1930 President Calvin Coolidge made the caves a National Park. Jim White was present at the dedication of the caverns. Jim named all the cave formations. Most were eerie names like "Devils Den", others like "Fairy Land" were named for their beauty. The bottomless pit at Carlsbad Caverns is one of those myths that get created over time. The hole really is only 140 feet deep and 280 feet to the top of the caverns roof, so it is a total of 420 feet tall – far from bottomless.

There are 18 species of bats living in Carlsbad Caverns. The most abundant are the Mexican Free Tailed Bat. Bats are one of the most diverse creatures on the planet. They live on every continent, other than Antarctica and some remote islands. They are the only flying mammals on Earth. They can vary in size from an adult's thumb to one species that have more than a five foot wing span! The reason the Mexican Bat is called free tailed is because most bats have a membrane between their tail and feet that is used when flying to catch insects and scoop up water to drink. Normally you wouldn't see anything past the membrane, but a Mexican Free Tailed Bat has a half inch tail that extends beyond the membrane.

My father, sisters, Samantha and Stephanie, and I left our home on Monday and drove to Las Vegas, New Mexico. This is not the famous gambling city in Nevada; this was a much smaller city in New Mexico. After spending the night there we drove to the White City RV resort outside the town of Carlsbad. Later that evening went to the caves and watched the bat flight at 7:15 PM. The bats that we saw were Mexican Free Tailed Bats. Their bodies are the size of a adult's thumb. The bat flight was amazing! At first we thought that the bat flight would be last very long because there was an initial first burst of bats that lasted only a few minutes. A short time later a major wave of bats came out of the caves in a seemingly never ending, upward spiraling circle of bats that lasted more then three hours. They were amazing!

The bats go out for their nightly feeding to the surrounding fields and valleys in search of bugs...Each of the more then four hundred thousand bats will eat its own weight in bugs every night. This provides a great service to the farmers and other people living in the area.

The next day we went down into the caverns. They were one of the most amazing things I have ever seen. Going into the caves was my favorite part of the whole trip. At first the caves were just a big, dark, deep hole, but once you get past the twilight zone there is so much to see that you become overwhelmed. After walking about one mile into the caves, there is one very "big room" that is the largest room in the cave system. It is called, what else, the Big Room. The Big Room is more then 8.2 acres, or more then six footballs fields in size.

We explored the caverns for about four hours. It was nice that we were able to leave the caves by using an elevator that the Park Service had installed; this made leaving the caverns much easier then hiking into them. The next day we started back home to Colorado

This trip taught me that often the size of things can be strongly influenced by our perception. For example, Cango Caves that I visited many years ago in South Africa are roughly the same size as Carlsbad Caverns. However, Cango Caves seemed much smaller because they did not have as many formations and did not seem as large or expansive. In Cango Caves there was often light in from the outside world, but in Carlsbad Caverns there was absolutely no light except from flashlights we carried and the small lamps along the trails. Carlsbad Caverns seemed so much larger and made me realize just how small I am in this great big world that we live in.

About The Author

Michael Raymond Brasier was born on May 16, 1993, in Franktown, Colorado (a very small town south of Denver). Michael has been fortunate to have had the opportunity to travel around the world and has visited thirteen different countries, so far.

Aside from his travels, Michael does his chores around the house and the property (he lives on approximately thirty acres). He also helps care for all of the family's animals, including three horse, seven ostriches, a goat named Charlie, and pond full of catfish and bluegill. He also makes many other contributions to the family and the property by helping with whatever projects are being worked on at the time, such as, building a new barn, clearing trees and brush, or planting vegetables in the greenhouse. Michael has also been home schooled since the third grade. Home schooling has afforded him the opportunity to travel and the flexibility to do other activities.

Michael has been very active in martial arts since he was six years old (1999). He was the Colorado State Champion in 2000 in his division for forms and was a four-time gold medalist at the State Games of Colorado in 2004. He also won a gold medal, national champion, in forms and bronze medal in weapons at the 2005 National Games. Michael is currently a brown belt in Tae Kwon Do (his last colored belt) and is working towards testing for his black belt sometime in 2006.

The author is also an avid scuba diver since obtaining his PADI Open Water Certification in May 2003. He has made over twenty-five dives so far, including dives in Cancun, Cozumel, Puerto Vallarta, the Cenotes in Mexico, and recently the Galapagos Islands.

Michael, like most kids his age, also enjoys playing X-Box, computer games, and riding his horse, Frank (so named because his horse has blue-eyes) through the woods where he lives.